RUN WITH THIS

3-Minute Daily Devotional

LEATTA MITCHELL

Copyright © 2023 by Leatta Mitchell.

Produced for Publication by
The Author's Pen, LLC
PO Box 16314
Fort Worth, Texas 76132
www.tapwriting.com

All rights are reserved.
No part of this publication may be reproduced, stored in a retrieval system, or transmitted, in any form or by any means, electronic, mechanical, photocopying, recording or otherwise, without the prior written permission of the publisher.

Run With This: 3-Minute Daily Devotional/ Leatta Mitchell.
-- 1st printed.
ISBN 978-1-948248-59-4
leattamitchell.com

Scripture taken from the (NKJV®) New King James Version®.
Copyright © 1982 by Thomas Nelson. Used by permission.
All rights reserved.

Scripture quotations marked (NIV) are taken from the Holy Bible, New International Version®, NIV®. Copyright © 1973, 1978, 1984, 2011 by Biblica, Inc.™ Used by permission of Zondervan. All rights reserved worldwide. www.zondervan.com The "NIV" and "New International Version" are trademarks registered in the United States Patent and Trademark Office by Biblica, Inc.™

Scripture quotations marked (NLT) are taken from the Holy Bible, New Living Translation, copyright ©1996, 2004, 2015 by Tyndale House Foundation. Used by permission of Tyndale House Publishers, Carol Stream, Illinois 60188.
All rights reserved.

Scripture quotations taken from the (NASB®) New American Standard Bible®, Copyright © 1960, 1971, 1977, 1995, 2020 by The Lockman Foundation. Used by permission.
All rights reserved. www.lockman.org

Scriptures marked KJV are taken from the KING JAMES VERSION (KJV): KING JAMES VERSION, public domain.

All Scripture marked with the designation "GW" is taken from GOD'S WORD®. © 1995, 2003, 2013, 2014, 2019, 2020 by God's Word to the Nations Mission Society. Used by permission.

ACKNOWLEDGMENTS

I dedicate this book to the person who needs to start over again. Or the person who realizes he or she needs a starting point in being encouraged, inspired, or a simple place to start studying God's word.

I want to thank my mother, Mrs. Leola B. Mitchell, and my father, the late Mack C. Mitchell, Sr., for always encouraging me and teaching me to trust in the Lord.

I also want to thank Apostle Sandra Harris and Obadiah's Court for helping with creating this book.

Blessings always.

CONTENTS

Acknowledgments 3
Forethought 7
Day 1: Chosen 9
Day 2: Thanking HIM 13
Day 3: I Have the Authority 17
Day 4: Holiness 21
Day 5: Your Words 25
Day 6: Salt 29
Day 7: Do It Afraid 33
Day 8: Imagination 37
Day 9: One Hundredfold 41
Day 10: What Are You Saying? 45
Day 11: Roaring Lion 49
Day 12: You 53
Day 13: Boomerang 57
Day 14: Our Father in Heaven 61
Day 15: Words 65
Day 16: Friends 69
Day 17: Daily Bread 73
Day 18: I Am 77

Day 19: The Lake	81
Day 20: The Donkey	85
Day 21: Just Because	89
Day 22: He is Provisional	93
Day 23: Wait For It	97
Day 24: You Choose	101
Day 25: He Even	105
Day 26: On Wings	109
Day 27: Promises	113
Day 28: His Love Language	117
Day 29: The Blessing	121
Day 30: O' Give Thanks	125
Bonus Devotional: It is a Choice	129
Afterthought	133

FORETHOUGHT

I was in Chuckie-Cheese many years ago celebrating and chaperoning my younger cousin's birthday party. There were several kids from 8 to 11 years old at the party. While sitting at the table with the other chaperons, I noticed the group of kids attempting to get their tickets out of the machine. I walked over and asked, "What are you all doing?" One of the kids said, "All of my tickets did not come out!" At that point, I noticed an attendant passing by and asked for assistance. The attendant could not solve the problem and was taking longer than the kids could tolerate. As a result, the kids were getting stirred up. I asked the attendant what could be done so the kids could continue to enjoy the birthday party.

All of a sudden, one of the eight-year-olds in the group stood strong like a soldier, stomping her foot while blurting out, "Get me the manager!" As I turned to look in amazement, I started smiling because she caught me off guard. In a millisecond, two thoughts raced through my mind, (1) I am the chaperone...lol and (2) she recognized we needed someone with more authority to help than this employee.

As humorous as this story is, it holds truths. This devotional is designed to get you to the manager of your life: Jesus Christ! I pray it reminds you to use the Word of God in managing your life by taking less time than grabbing a cup of coffee from your local barista— to get instructions and inspiration each day.

In 2018 and 2019, I needed someplace to restart. I had gone through heartbreaking challenges one after another, and in some respect, stopped trusting that God would come through. I remember being at Niagara Falls in Canada, crying and asking God to help me start again, and to trust Him again. As I pled to God, the Holy Spirit led me to small devotionals on YouTube or to bible-based devotional books. I write these devotionals as an opportunity to seed into your life the way devotionals have done for me. If you're looking to start again, find help and encouragement this is for you. If you're in need of inspiration or want a daily reminder to spend time with the Lord, this is for you.

Be blessed.

DAY 1
CHOSEN

Toni Braxton said, "Choosing a new chapter in life is not always easy, but you have to choose to be chosen!"

GUESS WHAT?

The Lord said in John 15:16 NIV, "You did not choose me, but I chose you and appointed you so that you might go and bear fruit—fruit that would last—and so that whatever you ask in my name the Father will give you."

Regardless of who chooses you or wants you in their life, find rest and comfort in knowing you are chosen by the Highest King that ever lived… Jesus Christ! You can be assured that no matter who leaves or stays in your life, you are and will always be chosen by God.

Prayer: *Thank you, Lord, that you see me when others don't. I adore you because according to John 15:16, you see and choose me. I find comfort in knowing you will never leave me or forsake me. Thank You, Lord, that my life is blessed because you chose me!*

RUN with this today:

The Lord Chooses YOU

DAY 2
THANKING HIM

So often, we wait for people to become accepting of us, show gratitude toward us, and honor us only to find ourselves disappointed when that does not happen or does not occur to the magnitude we believe it should. One day, while accepting an award, a famous rapper started thanking himself for various things. At first, one could start laughing and thinking, what kind of foolishness is this? Later, after thinking about his gratitude toward himself, I pondered reasons he would thank himself. Perhaps, there were times he wanted to give up, but he pushed to accomplish his dreams. Maybe he fought against believing negative thoughts about himself or the negative opinions of others. At any rate, I began to reflect on the ways I could be thankful for the things I've overcome, too. I owe my thanks to God.

Psalms 9:1 NLT:

"I will praise you, LORD, with all my heart; I will tell of all the marvelous things you have done."

Here is the start of my thank you list:

- **Thank you**, Lord, for guiding me.
- **Thank you,** Lord, for loving me.
- **Thank you,** Lord, for healing my bruised soul after my divorce.
- **Thank you,** Lord, for your protection and for being a provider to me.
- **Thank you,** Lord, for holding my hand and guiding me through every step.
- **Thank you,** Lord, for keeping me safe as I travel the world.

Prayer: *Sovereign Lord, thank you for everything. Amen!*

RUN with this today:

YOU owe the LORD a big, huge THANK YOU.

So, take a minute, write them down, and give it to Him!

DAY 3
I HAVE THE AUTHORITY

I'm reminded of a time when my father had a stroke and the Lord allowed him to walk away unscathed. Weeks into his recovery, while sitting at the dinner table during a family gathering, I went on a mild tirade about what he needed to do and not do in order to maintain his wellness and prevent another stroke. I told him to take his medication on time, not eat certain foods, and exercise three times a week. Interrupting me mid-sentence, my niece said to my mother matter-of-factly, "Maw-Maw, she is not even a doctor!" Everyone erupted in laughter.

Essentially, she was saying I did not have the authority to tell her grandfather, MY FATHER, what he should and should not be doing to stay healthy.

But unlike the above scenario, YOU have the authority to command things in your world as you are made in the image and likeness of Christ.

Psalms 33:9 NLT says, "For when He spoke, the world began! It appeared at His command."

Prayer: *Thank you, Mighty God. I adore you because you made me in your image, which gave me the power to command things and situations to align with your Word. Father, even when things look impossible, please let me not forget that I have the power to speak to things and change situations. I love you immensely. Amen!*

RUN with this today:

So, what are you COMMANDING?!

Are you commanding your health to align with the Word of God? Or is it your finances, your relationships, or your life? God gave you the power to do whatever it is, so get to commanding!

DAY 4
HOLINESS

> *"Holiness is always right!"*
> —Jackie Hill Perry

Holiness means to be set apart and sacred. Set apart for service unto God.

"Being holy" or "living holy" is first about our heart's posture with God, and then our behaviors follow it. When your heart is set on doing what is right before God and holding up to the standards of God, you are fulfilling 2 Corinthians 7:1b NLT, which says, "And let us work toward complete holiness because we fear God."

> **Prayer:** *Perfect God, my desire is to live a life that is holy. I ask that you steer me in the path of holiness through your Word. Help my life be set apart and acceptable to you. Amen!*

RUN with this today:

Holiness is always right, even when it's not what we want to do; it is right because that is what our Heavenly Father calls us to be!

DAY 5
YOUR WORDS

I LOVE THE GOLDEN GIRLS! For those not familiar, The Golden Girls was a popular television series in the 80s centered around four older women doing life together. I have watched every single episode at least ten times, each time as if it's the first time. I have shirts, and I DVR them as if I believe Hallmark Network will suddenly stop playing them!

In one episode, Sophia (the oldest character and mother to Dorothy) and her daughter, Dorothy, attended the wedding of the daughter of one of Sophia's old friends. When Sophia sees an old friend, she places a curse on him from a vendetta between them fifty years earlier. As a result, every time something happened that suggested her "curse" had taken effect, she would shimmy her shoulders and gloat with an "I told you so" smirk on her face. Dorothy laughed it off and told her, "Ma, you are being ridiculous!"

Throughout the wedding, strange things were happening like his socks falling, spilling juice on his shirt, and his daughter even considered calling off the wedding. Although this is a television show, the character believed her words had the power. And as Christians, while we do not manifest evil, this episode highlighted a belief that **words can make things happen. And even if you do not believe your own words, you CAN believe every jot and tittle of the Word of God!**

The Golden Girls was a scripted American sitcom with well-developed characters and plots, produced for entertainment. Conversely, you are a real person with God's Word hidden in your heart and you have His angelic host on guard, ready to do His bidding. So, let me challenge you to ask yourself what you want to accomplish in life. Next, find a promise in the Word of God, and hold on to it until it manifests, trusting that His Word cannot lie!

Job 22:28 KJV says, "Thou shalt also decree a thing, and it shall be established."

My Pastor, Apostle Charles Perry, Jr., teaches believers should, "Make God's Word HEAVY," and believe it regardless of how long it takes to manifest.

Prayer: *Lord, I decree today that I make your Word heavy in my life because you have said that heaven and earth shall pass away, but your Word shall remain. Father, I will mimic your Son and my big brother, Jesus Christ. Jesus said he only says what his Father says. Lord, help me live by that and give me feet of steel that I may not move off your Word until I hold your promises. Amen!*

RUN with this today:

He is not a man who should lie or come void of His Word!!!

DAY 6
SALT

I was looking at the news one night and watched many people who lacked morals, were indecent towards people in how they treated others, or whose thinking vibrated at a shallow level, and my heart became heavy for a moment.

The next morning during prayer, I began with:

Good morning, Jesus, what ever happened to decent and good-hearted people who are not out for themselves? Before I could finish my thought, I heard the Holy Spirit say:

"BUT YOU ARE THE SALT OF THE EARTH, AND YOU CAN'T LET THEM CHANGE YOU!"

I sat with this truth for a moment. Although I wanted to complete my rant, the Holy Spirit quieted my heart because He was right!

A bird flies in the air, a whale swims in the ocean, and you are a child of the King, designed to walk the earth, leaving dribbles of salt. These bits of salt are evidenced by your peace, unity, goodness, smiling at people, helping others, being kind, and in the many ways that God's Word is felt through your actions.

Matthew 5:13 NIV reads, "You are the salt of the earth. But how can the salt be made salty again if it loses its saltiness? It is no longer good for anything except to be thrown out and trampled underfoot."

> **Prayer:** *Holy Spirit, you made me in your image. You also said I was the salt of the earth, but if the salt lost its savor, how would it be made salty again? It would be suitable for nothing. Father, thank you for preserving me and reminding me that one of my Kingdom jobs on earth is to be the salt. Holy One, help me always to represent the Kingdom of Heaven, leaving dribbles of salt by living out Godliness everywhere I go. Amen!*

RUN with this today:

Shake your salt of peace, salt of love, salt of kindness, and most importantly, salt of God's Word everywhere you go today!

DAY 7
DO IT AFRAID

During a conversation, an acquaintance shared with me some of the things that were bothering her, and how she was processing that the only way she was going to get any results was to step into the unknown, trust her faith, and do something about what was bothering her. She kept saying things like, "I'm nervous, I'm afraid, and I'm unsure!" As I listened, I blurted, "So what? Do it afraid! Even if it doesn't work out how you want, you would not have allowed fear to control you!"

And as sure as the bible is true and you reap what you sow, one morning, I told the same person I was avoiding a hard conversation with someone.

I was still determining how the person would react and felt uncertain about the conversation. She interrupted me and said, "There was a lady months ago that told me, 'Sometimes, you have to do things afraid.'" She continued, "So, I'm using her exact words, 'So What? Do It Afraid!'"

Fear is often horrible; it is one of the enemy's devices to hold us back and make us doubt God and ourselves. I love Joshua 1:9b NIV because it commands us to, "...be strong and courageous. Do not be afraid; do not be discouraged, for the Lord your God will be with you wherever you go."

I want to empower you, as you read these words to take whatever fear you have, whether it is about an ailment, relationships, or financial issues, to God in prayer. Trust God for the courage to go through, take the fear away, and face the situation head-on, because YOU ARE AN OVERCOMER!

> **Prayer:** *Holy One, thank you that out of your love for me, you commanded me in Joshua 1:9 to be strong and courageous. Do not be afraid; do not be discouraged, for the Lord your God will be with you wherever you go. Thank you for saying you had not given me a spirit of fear but of love, joy, and a sound mind. Father, whenever fear creeps in, please allow the Word that I have hidden in my heart to come like a rushing wind and blow it away. I love you so much. In Jesus' name.*

RUN with this today:

You have to trust in something or someone. Why not trust God knowing that He said, "I am with you and will protect you wherever you go" (Genesis 28:15)?

DAY 8
IMAGINATION

Cindy Trimm is one of the greatest blessings the Lord has given humanity with, and she is also one of my self-proclaimed prayer mentors! She often says, "Your feet will never take you where your mind/imagination doesn't take you first!"

In my meditation and imaging time, I envisioned opening a Residential Treatment Center where kids in the foster care system would live. I mentally used the image of one of the facilities I had worked in years ago. I did not want to own this particular facility, but I needed an image in my mind during my meditation time. I imagined myself driving to it, kids greeting me, and having a ribbon-cutting ceremony. While exercising one day, I received a call as if out of thin air, and it was someone connected with the facility. She asked me if I wanted to buy or rent it from them because they were no longer occupying the building.

I was wholly tickled and amazed because no one knew I was using the building during my meditation time, nor did I know the facility was closing. I manifested or brought it to me through imagination. Genesis 13:14-15 says concerning God's promise to Abram, and I'm paraphrasing, as far as you can see, you will permanently possess it.

I ask, "What do you see for yourself tomorrow, five years, or even ten years from now?" Bring it to God to perfect the picture for you. I want you to do two things: see it for yourself, and then bring it to the Lord and let him figure out the details. Psalms 138:8 KJV says, "He perfects that which concerns you!"

> **Prayer:** *Holy One, you are so outstandingly remarkable in all things. Father, thank you for vision and the ability to see and have life more abundantly, to the full and overflow. Thank you for opening my eyes to new possibilities in you and receiving your blessings. Abraham declared he was an old man, but I had been blessed in every way. I now decree and declare that you are blessing me in every way. In Jesus' name.*

RUN with this today:

Whatever you see for your life, imagine you possess it, and bring it to God. But, do not let the image go until it has become a real thing in your life!

DAY 9
ONE HUNDREDFOLD

Often, we hear individuals asking for an increase in their lives in various places. The Bible gives us an example of how to ask for a hundredfold blessing. Pray this scripture over your life starting today!

It is from Genesis 26:12-14 NIV.

"Isaac planted crops in that land and the same year reaped a hundredfold, because the Lord blessed him. The man became rich, and his wealth continued to grow until he became very wealthy. He had so many flocks and herds and servants that the Philistines envied him."

Father, I decree and declare that I, (YOUR NAME _____), have sown in the land and receive in the same year a hundred-fold because you blessed me. And I, (YOUR NAME _____), am rich, and my wealth continues to grow, making me very wealthy. I had so many (list what you want from God) _____

_____
_____
_____
_____ and a great store of everything and I am envied by those that do not call you Lord.

> **Prayer:** *Holy God, you are extraordinary. You are the triune God that deserves to be worshipped. Father, your Word says that Isaac sowed in the land and received in the same year a hundred-fold, and you blessed him. You are not a respecter of person, and per your Word, I use these exact words as a blessing over my life. In Jesus' name.*

RUN with this today:

The Lord wants you to seek Him First; then all these things shall be added unto you!!

DAY 10
WHAT ARE YOU SAYING?

When my niece was younger, we'd often have slumber parties. I vividly remember one sleepover when she was four-years-old. We had our usual movie night with snacks on hand, eating and drinking everything in sight. After falling asleep, I was awakened by her squirming in the middle of the night. I looked to investigate the sound, and she was looking right at me. She says, "Aunt Etta, I sweat on myself," pointing to her midsection. LOL.

She confused her words. She was trying to communicate that she had urinated on herself, but used the word sweat instead.

When I compare my sweet little niece in this example to our walk with the Lord, I can only imagine the words we are saying to ourselves to describe what's happening in our lives that God never spoke about us. That is, using words with negative and defeated meanings like you are ugly, you are stupid, you will never accomplish anything, and you will forever lose in life. They are, in essence, causing us to be confused about who we are.

But the truth is, His thoughts of you are for good and not evil (towards you), and HE wants to give you hope and a future! (Jeremiah 29:11)

Here are a few words HE SAID about you:

- As far as you can see, you can permanently possess it (Genesis 13:14-18, New Living Translation Version)
- You are fearfully and wonderfully made (Psalm 139:14, New International Version)
- Like Jacob, you are a special possession (Deuteronomy 32:9, Amplified Version)
- You are the apple of His eye (Psalms 18:7, Contemporary English Version)
- I am for you (Psalms 56:9, English Standard Version)

So, I admonish you, distinguish His Words from the wrong words. Know what your Father thinks of you! Even if it appears differently or resembles a mirage at a glance, always remember to do what Jesus would do or say. He said, *I Only to Say What My Father Says* (John 12:49).

Prayer: *Spirit of the Living God, thank you for speaking definite things over me through the love letter you left for me, the Holy Bible. Please allow the Comforter to remind me to say only Words from the Father. In Jesus' name.*

RUN with this today:

The LORD thinks well of me and wants me to have the absolute best in every area of my life!

DAY 11
ROARING LION

1 Peter 5:8 NLT says, "The devil prowls around **LIKE** a roaring lion seeking whom he can devour."

I have read and heard of this scripture many times, but this time, the word, **LIKE**, stuck out like a sunflower amongst red roses...WOW!

By definition, the word *like* means similar to, but not the exact thing (Macmillan Dictionary). My mother has twenty-two siblings, but one in particular looks like my mother's twin. They are identical in their walk, look, size, how they wear their hair, how they hold their lips, and some of their thinking patterns. They are five years apart, but you could instantly take them for twins when you see them together. Although they look alike, they are very different when you put them side-by-side.

What has taken on "the look *like*" *or* comes at you "*like a roaring lion*?" Put it next to God and then compare. Despite how it roars, you will quickly find it is not a real lion, just a mirage!

> **Prayer:** *Lord, I thank you that you are a battle axe and have been my weapon of war. I am truly grateful that things only look like but are not. Father, help me take everything and compare it to your Word to help me decide if the situation is or if it only looks like it. In Jesus' name.*

RUN with this today:

> **Don't let counterfeit lions or the roar of life's circumstances fool you! It is not even a real lion; it only looks like one!**

DAY 12
YOU

"It's what you say to yourself that heals you."
—TD Jakes

YOU are your loudest voice!!! Never forget that! So say amazing things to yourself!

> **Prayer:** *Loving Father, I have not always said things about myself that were healing. Sometimes, the words I spoke about myself were outright mean and false. I cancel and curse every word and thought spoken by me over my life that was not the truth and can't be backed up in the Word of God! I thank you that the Holy Spirit alerts me every time I say something about myself that is contrary to your word. In Jesus' name.*

RUN with this today:

Despite past mistakes and moments of weakness, I will say excellent things about ME!

DAY 13
BOOMERANG

One morning, I was praying from Isaiah 55:11 KJV, which reads, "So shall your Word be that goes forth out of my mouth and it shall not return unto me void." Out of nowhere, I heard the Spirit of the Lord say, "Like a boomerang." I immediately started researching the word boomerang. According to the Oxford Language Dictionary, it as a curved flat piece of wood that can be thrown so that it will return to the thrower. To my surprise, I saw several pictures and YouTube videos of people throwing a boomerang and waiting for it to return to them.

Let me show you how. Imagine these things with me:

- The boomerang is the WORD of God.
- Releasing the boomerang (the WORD of God) out of your mouth is your faith in the fact that it is going to return to you.

- Standing there waiting for it to return symbolizes the process you would go through between speaking the Word of God and waiting for it to produce what you spoke!

That is precisely what happened in the videos of the boomerang being thrown. The person stood still, watching with full expectation and excitement that the boomerang they had thrown out would return to them. So, whenever you SPEAK out of the Word of God, believing His Word will not come back void; you will have what you say.

> **Prayer:** *Lord, you said your Word would not return to me void but will accomplish its purpose! Thank you, Lord, that You are a firm foundation, and I find Sarah's account of you true; that you are reliable, trustworthy, and true to your Word. In Jesus' name.*

RUN with this today:

In one of the videos, one man was throwing a boomerang and couldn't make it come back to him. He started saying things like forget it, this is crazy, and what is the problem? And consequently, the boomerang never returned to him. It would fall halfway, or it would not fly far at all. Perhaps because he became frustrated and started speaking negatively. **Please don't be like this man**. Instead, keep watching, praying, and monitoring what you are saying, and watch His Word accomplish what you are waiting for!

DAY 14
OUR FATHER IN HEAVEN

I was thinking about the principles of prayer while listening to a sermon on the topic of prayer. One of the critical principles of prayer is adoration! Adoration is simply praising God for who He is and showing honor and respect.

When Jesus was teaching the disciples to pray to the Lord, He used a specific adjective to describe who the Lord is, and that's the word *hallowed. By* definition, it means holy, sacred, and set apart. (Merriam-Webster Dictionary)

When Jesus said hallowed in the prayer, He taught them the importance of adoring God first. Read Jesus' adornment to the Father by replacing the word hallowed with the words in parenthesis as this:

- Our Father in Heaven (sacred) be your name,
- Or our Father in Heaven (Holy) be your name,

- Or our Father in Heaven (consecrated) be your name,
- Or our Father in Heaven (honored) be your name.

You can see the praise He offered God. Throughout your day, **describe who** the Lord is to you and watch the Spirit of the Lord rush in to give you his attention!

- Lord, you are great.
- Lord, you wiped my tears away.
- Lord, you are a winner.
- Lord, you are my champion.
- Lord, you love me unfailingly.
- Lord, you are my battle axe.
- Lord, you are my company keeper.
- Lord, you are terrific.
- Lord, your love is amazing.
- Lord, you are strong and fierce.
- Lord, you are a great advocate for me.

YOUR TURN.

Lord, you are_____, _____, and _____.

Prayer: *Father, you are a great God, I worship you and call you Holy. Father, in the model prayer that Jesus taught the disciples, He instructed that your name be kept hallowed or holy. Thank you for being a holy, righteous God who loves me with unfailing love. I worship your name! In Jesus' name.*

RUN with this today:

Create a list of words today that honor God. Use the list below until you develop your own.

Awesome; wonderful; great one; holy; extraordinary; my peace; best friend; protector; provider; lovely; most High; my keeper
JUST HONOR HIM; HE DESERVES IT!

DAY 15
WORDS

"A gentle answer turns away wrath, but a harsh word stirs up anger. The tongue of the wise adorns knowledge, but the mouth of the fool gushes folly." (Proverbs 15:1-2 NIV).

Which type of person are you? A wise person or a fool?

Hint: You can tell by your words and how you respond to things!

> **Prayer:** *Holy God, you said in Proverbs that He who walks with wise men would be wise, But the companion of fools will suffer harm. Father, let me choose wise companions and friendships. Teach me to speak softly so I won't stir up wrath. In Jesus' name.*

RUN with this today:

Would the Lord be pleased with the things that come from my mouth?

DAY 16
FRIENDS

Over several days, the Holy Spirit kept telling me, "Watch the friends you are hanging around, and do not get involved with the wrong people because there is destruction behind it."

This prompted me to study the closest friends of Jesus: Peter, James, and John. These three were with Jesus at two pivotal points in His life. He chose them to be with Him in pain and at one of the noted pinnacle moments of Jesus' ministry.

First, when He was in the Garden of Gethsemane. Matthew 26:36-37 NIV states: "Then Jesus brought them to a garden grove, Gethsemane, and told them to sit down and wait while He went ahead to pray. He took Peter with Him and Zebedee's two sons, James and John, and began to be filled with anguish and despair."

The second time Jesus chose these three to be with Him was at the Mount of Transfiguration. Mark

9:2 NIV states: "'Jesus took Peter, James, and John with Him and led them up a high mountain, where they were all alone. There, He was transfigured before them."

In one moment, He was about to live through His most painful time, and the other moment, He went through a transfiguration and changed right before their eyes.

After studying Jesus' relationship with these men, I started paying attention. I reevaluated people in my life that would face both good and bad times with me. The ones I could not count on showing up, I repositioned them in my life! And not because they are bad people; they just don't belong in the inner courts of my life. I want to encourage you to do the same! Always remember meaningless relationships hold no gain for you; they just take up space!

Prayer: *To the God that sits high and looks low, I worship you! Father, allow me to choose friends that will sharpen me like iron sharpens iron. Please make me aware of my friendships because your Word declares bad company will corrupt good character. Give me a discerning heart so I choose wisely when bringing others into the inner courts of my life. In Jesus' name.*

RUN with this today:

Ask the Lord to show you your friendships and give you the wisdom to know their positions in your life.

DAY 17
DAILY BREAD

I had taken a loaf of bread from my parent's house because I did not want to stop at the grocery store. As I was driving, I saw a homeless lady wrapped in a blanket at the corner of the street asking for food as cars passed. The light turned red, and my car stopped in front of her. I rolled the window down and offered her the loaf of bread, as this was all I had. She held it up after I gave it to her and said, "Thank you, Lord, for my daily bread!" She was asking for food, I gave her food, and the first thing she did was honor God. This is an example for us all. Whether we are in lack or plenty, our first response should always yield honor to God.

I immediately thought of the scripture in Psalms 34:1 KJV, "I will bless the Lord at all times; His praise shall continually be in my mouth."

Prayer: *God, you are Holy, and I bless your name! In Jesus' name.*

RUN with this today:

Bless the Lord today!

DAY 18
I AM

While I was grocery shopping, this gorgeous little girl was singing a song as loud as she could. With everyone watching, she sang as if she was on Broadway. The words to her song were: **I am stronger, I am taller, and I am on my way!** She sang those words over and over.

I started smiling at her, and her mother said to me softly, "She sings this all day!" The next thing I knew, I unconsciously started humming her tune while standing in line, then I started singing it as I got in my car, and now I am writing it in this book so you can sing or say them as well.

The Bible says in Proverbs 18:21 ESV, "Death and life are in the power of the tongue, and those who love it will eat its fruit." This little girl is producing great fruit in her life with her own words. We should use her words that they also produce fruit for us!

Prayer: *Holy God, you said I could decree a thing which shall be established on the earth. I decree and declare that I am stronger, taller, soar on the wings of eagles, and on my way to the promises you have laid before me. In Jesus' name.*

RUN with this today:

If you don't want to see it in your life, don't say it!

DAY 19
THE LAKE

I walk around a lake at least three times a week. I have walked around this lake for several years! While walking one day, I saw these big, brownish eyes emerge reminding me of what looked like an alligator, and then suddenly, they went back into the water.

I later passed a man who had walked out by that lake for many more years than I, and asked, "Have you ever seen an alligator in this water?" He laughed and said, "No, I have lived around this lake for about 17 years; nothing is in this water!" So, I CONVINCED myself that what I had seen was not true.

About two months later, I was walking around the same lake, and I looked out in the water, and **indeed**, there was an alligator swimming in the water.

Later that night, I thought to myself how I convinced myself months earlier that I had not seen what I knew I had seen. I had trusted someone who had not seen what I saw. Instantly, the Holy Spirit said, "What else have you convinced yourself you have not seen when I have shown you already, despite people telling you it cannot happen?" In Genesis 13:14-17, the Lord gave Abram a vision of what He would possess in his life. Abram did not question it; he followed the instructions that he would possess the land after receiving the vision.

Don't be like me with the alligator. Knowing you saw something but allowing someone else to talk you out of what you had seen. If God gave you a vision, a dream, or a word, just believe it!

Prayer: *Thank you, Lord! Father, teach me what you have prepared for me, placed in my heart, and shown me in dreams or visions to hold on to despite what others say. Father, let me trust your Word as I arise and walk. In Jesus' name.*

RUN with this today:

Arise and walk. Your God promised destiny is at hand!

DAY 20
THE DONKEY

I was studying the Bible one day and stumbled on Numbers 22:28-31. Verse 28 (GW) states: "Then the LORD made the donkey speak, and it asked Balaam, 'What have I done to make you hit me three times?'"

I pondered that scripture for several minutes and started smiling; I found it very encouraging. I started thinking about my life and became quite joyful. If the Lord can make a donkey speak and hold a conversation with a human being, He can also bless me to have divine health, increase my finances, and bless me to live a long prosperous life. Now, your turn!

If the Lord can make a donkey speak, can't He also do

(x) _____,
(y) _____, and
(z) _____ for you?!

Go ahead, write it down!!!

Prayer: *Holy One, how great are you in all the earth! Thank you for reassuring me through your Word that nothing is impossible for you. Father, I trust you because you have Almighty power and can handle my concerns. I bless your name! In Jesus' name.*

RUN with this today:

He has all the power! And that's in Heaven and Earth!

DAY 21
JUST BECAUSE

The Father in Heaven loves you JUST BECAUSE and **not** BECAUSE OF…

NOTHING you can do will make Him love you any less or any more. He already loves you **supremely**!

Jeremiah 31:3a NIV says:

The Lord appeared to us in the past saying: "I have loved you with an everlasting love; I have drawn you with unfailing kindness."

> **Prayer:** *Lord, you are a great God! Thank you for loving me when I was not good to myself. And your love is not contingent on anything but because you do. I love you, Holy God! In Jesus' name.*

RUN with this today:

You will never find another love like this!

DAY 22
HE IS PROVISIONAL

While in Hawaii, I was sitting outside looking at the most beautiful blue and turquoise waters one can behold. As I listened to the sound of the water, lost in my thoughts, a couple passed by and threw breadcrumbs on the lawn. Seconds later, two birds swooped down, grabbing the food and flew away.

At that moment, the Holy Spirit brought this scripture back to my heart found in Matthew 6:26 NIV. It reads, "Look at the birds of the air, for they neither sow nor do they reap, nor do they gather into barns; and your Heavenly Father feeds them. Are you not much of more value than they?"

The birds did not know where their next provision was coming from. They watched and waited. Like our feathered friends in Hawaii, your Heavenly Father works on your behalf, as well. He is developing and orchestrating people for the right time and unknown to you who will provide what you need and carry you to the next stage of your God given destiny. But you have to mimic the birds. You must keep trusting, watching, and waiting for provision, and know the Lord will not forget you.

> **Prayer:** *Thank you, God, for being fantastic and fabulous! When I think about how birds go about their day-to-day movements without one care, let them become my example in trusting you will take care of me. Thank you for perfecting everything that concerns me and bringing everything into perfect alignment with your Word. In Jesus' name.*

RUN with this today:

He is perfecting everything that concerns you... believe it!

DAY 23
WAIT FOR IT

When she was younger, my niece had to undergo several major medical tests. Her parents promised her before a particular medical examination day that if she cooperated well with the medical team at the appointment, they would reward her by taking her to her favorite restaurant and a movie of her choice.

Every test the team needed to complete she cooperated with them without any push back. After the appointment, she visited her favorite restaurant and had a marvelous time. After eating, she and her parents returned home. Her mother was in the kitchen, and her father was on the phone. Her mother looked to see what she was doing, and my niece was sitting on the top of the stairs with her elbows on her knees and little hands pressed against her face with a sad puppy look on her face.

Her mother asked her what was wrong, and she said, "I guess y'all promised me for nothing!" About that time, her father hung up the phone and asked his wife what was wrong, and once she told him, he interjected. "We took you to your favorite restaurant and got you a toy!" She said to him, still sitting in the same place, "I know, thank you, but you promised me a movie." And her father told her, "Right, but the movie you chose does not come out until tomorrow." Her mother said, "Yeah, and we already purchased tickets to go!" Without a second thought, my niece jumped up and screamed with excitement!

How often do we ask God for something, and He promises we will have it, but it doesn't happen on our timetable? As a result, we pout, become distant from Him, and ask for explanations of when and why.

2 Peter 3:8b NIV, says, "With the Lord a day is like a thousand years, and a thousand years is like a day." Benson's Commentary[1] noted, "In one moment, he (God) could do the work of a thousand years; therefore, he is *not slow,* he is always equally able, equally ready to fulfill his promise; *and a thousand years,* yea, the longest time, is no more delay to the eternal God *than one day* is to us." Isn't that amazing? Sometimes, one of the hardest things to do is trust God's timing! **I KNOW!** But because He loves us so much, he works it all for

---

[1] Benson's Commentary can be located: https://www.studylight.org/commentaries/eng/rbc/2-peter-3.html

our good; He already has everything planned out and is dispatching angels to help bring everything to life for us!

> **Prayer:** *Father of the universe, thank you for having me on your mind so much that you said your thoughts of me outnumber the sand on the seashore. Thank you that your promises are yes and amen! Instead of pouting or doubting your Word because you can't lie, I will remind you to remember everything you promised me and stand fast until it manifests. In Jesus' name.*

RUN with this today:

Ask the Holy Spirit to help you trust the Lord's timing!

DAY 24
YOU CHOOSE

You Choose the Life You Want by the Words You Speak, So CHOOSE Your Words Wisely

Some things are factual, and some things are true.

What is true always lines up with the Word of God.

The Bible tells us in John 14:6 NIV, the Lord is, "the way, the truth, and the life."

Whenever we speak, we should always speak the truth regardless of the facts of a matter.

Here are a few facts vs. "true" statements:

- Fact: I lost a job vs. true statement.

  In all these things, You are more than a conqueror (Romans 8:37 KJV).
- Fact: I failed at things in life or I am a poor communicator vs. true statement.

  You are well able to overcome it and possess it (Numbers 13:30 NKJV).

- Fact: I believe I do not equal up to other people vs. true statement.

  You are fearfully and wonderfully made (Psalms 139:14 KJV).

- Fact: I do not have any talent or any way to make extra money vs. true statement.

  HE gives you the ability to produce wealth (Deuteronomy 8:18 NIV).

- Fact: I have been sick in my body vs. true statement.

  HE will restore your health and heals your wounds (Jeremiah 30:17 Berean Study Bible).

Prayer: *Holy One, thank you that you are the truth. Father, let me choose my words based on the validity and reliability of your Word. Please forgive me for the times I have spoken words contrary to what you have ordained. In Jesus' name.*

RUN with this today:

Choose the words released from your mouth.

DAY 25
HE EVEN

Mark 7:31-37 (NLT)

31 Jesus left Tyre and went up to Sidon before returning to the Sea of Galilee and the region of the Ten Towns.

32 A deaf man with a speech impediment was brought to him, and the people begged Jesus to lay his hands on the man to heal him.

33 Jesus led him away from the crowd so they could be alone. He put his fingers into the man's ears. Then, spitting on his own fingers, he touched the man's tongue.

34 Looking up to heaven, he sighed and said, "Ephphatha," which means, "Be opened!"

35 Instantly the man could hear perfectly, and his tongue was freed so he could speak plainly!

36 Jesus told the crowd not to tell anyone, but the more he told them not to, the more they spread the news.

37 *They were utterly amazed and repeatedly said, "Everything he does is wonderful. He even makes the deaf to hear and gives speech to those who cannot speak."*

This is a conversation among the people of that city who witnessed the miracle, marveling at what happened. Like when you experience something astonishing, in your excitement, you call and tell everyone. Overtaken by amazement, they began naming things one by one. What stuck out was when the people in the city said he even heals the deaf and mute. The word EVEN denotes that He (Christ) had done MORE than they'd seen!

What is your *even*...? _____!

Here are some of mine:

- He **even** healed my heart.
- He **even** has given me peace.
- He **even** blessed me with financial resources.
- He **even** blessed me with good health.
- He **even** made my mother well.
- He **even** used me to write this book.

Prayer: *Magnificent God, thank you for continually blessing me. I worship you and honor you. Forgive me for not always acknowledging the 'even' things you have done. In Jesus' name.*

RUN with this today:

Think about your *even* throughout the day.

DAY 26
ON WINGS

Isaiah 40:31 NLT: "But those who trust in the LORD will find new strength. They will soar high on wings like eagles. They will run and not grow weary. They will walk and not faint."

> **Prayer:** *Lord, thank you that I am trusting in you, and even more, thank you, Lord, for saying I would mount up on the wings as eagles. Great God, thank you for allowing me to soar to new heights in everything I do. Thank you, Lord, that you are causing me to excel in places on eagles' wings and have given me the strength to run the distance for what you said I could have. I decree that I will not grow weary, disinterested, or give up. Lord, allow me to walk steadily, consistently, diligently, and not faint. Thank you, God, for being the great I am! In Jesus' name.*

RUN with this today:

Ask the Lord to take you to new heights in Him.

DAY 27
PROMISES

---

2 Corinthians 1:20 NIV, "For no matter how many promises God has made, they are "Yes" in Christ. And so through Him, the "Amen" is spoken by us to the glory of God."

All God's promises are yes and amen!

I am no different than you and every person who will read this book. There are moments when things look bleak for me. There are moments when I feel defeated. There are moments when I can't believe certain things have not occurred in my life.

In those moments, I remind myself **God CANNOT lie,** and then I remind myself of His promises to me!

Prayer: *Father, thank you that you make promises, but even more, that you keep your promises. I thank you, God you said, "You will not break your covenant, nor will you alter the words that come out of your lips!" Your WORDS are true, and I love that I can count on them. In Jesus' name. (See Psalms 89:34 KJV)*

RUN with this today:

Find a promise in His Word and hold him to it until it manifests!!!!!

DAY 28
HIS LOVE LANGUAGE

One of the beautiful aspects of a new relationship is the gift of learning the person. Their likes and dislikes. Sharing exciting moments, and most importantly, coming to understand their love language(s). There's a similar excitement when you are in a relationship with Jesus Christ! When you spend time with Him, He teaches you His love languages and introduces you to new things about Him.

One of Jesus's love languages is **praise**. Psalms 22:3 says, and I'm paraphrasing, "How the Father is Holy and enthroned and how he inhabits the praise of his people." Inhabit in Hebrew means to dwell. He lives in and loves your praise towards him. Your praise is irresistible to God!

Make a habit of telling God how great He is, how wonderful He is, how He makes your heart sing, how loyal He is, and how outstanding He is!

Then, watch Him turn His face to shine upon you (favor you), and be gracious to you (give you peace). Numbers 6:26 NIV

Prayer: *Father, how awesome are you! Holy Father, forever let praise be on my lips for you because you are worthy of all the praise. In Jesus' name.*

RUN with this today:

Don't forget to praise Him!

DAY 29
THE BLESSING

Prayer: *Father, I know you to be strong and mighty; I know your love is exceptional and extraordinary because I have experienced it in my life. Holy God, you are every bit wonderful, patient, and generous, and because of your generosity and love towards me, you have spoken blessings over my life. Father, thank you for blessing me and being the creator of my life, and for also being the author and finisher of my faith.*

I Am that I Am, thank you for blessing me and enlarging my territory, and for keeping your hand upon me to keep me from all hurt, harm, and danger. God, I am so incredibly blessed and thankful that you said you have sent your Word out to heal me and deliver me from destruction, and you will have me prosper and be in good health even as my soul prospers.

Daddy, thank you for blessing me exceedingly, abundantly above all things that I can ask or think, and you love me so much that you are giving me the power to bring them to life. Worthy King, I worship you for filling my life with good things so that my youth will be renewed like an eagle, and on top of that, you are increasing me thousands of times more and blessing me as you promised you would. I will continue to worship you, Righteous God, for blessing my life in every way, and because you have come I may have a life to the full and overflow.

Amazing God, you have richly blessed me by promising me no evil will befall me, and that no plague will come near my dwelling, for you have given your angels charge over me to keep me in all my ways. Thank you, Lord, for being so mindful of me, and I ask if I have missed the mark in any way that you would forgive me and help me live my life as I am the child of The Triune God, and I worship you. In Jesus' name.

Reference Verses:

- Hebrews 12:2 (NKJV)
- 1 Chronicles 4:10 (NIV)
- Psalms 107:20 (ESV)
- 3 John 1:2 (NKJV)
- Ephesians 3:20 (Berean Literal Bible)
- Psalms 103:5 (NIV)
- Gen 24:1 (NLT)
- John 10:10 (NIV)
- Psalms 91:11 (NKJV)

RUN with this today:

You are blessed!

DAY 30
O' GIVE THANKS

Truthful God, your Word says give thanks to the Lord, for He is good, for His loving-kindness lasts forever. Give thanks to the God of gods, for His loving-kindness lasts forever. Give thanks to the Lord of lords, for His loving-kindness lasts forever. Give thanks to Him, who alone does great works, for His loving-kindness lasts forever. Give thanks to Him, who by wisdom made the heavens, for His loving-kindness lasts forever, and Lord, I agree.

Father, I give you thanks because you have been my leaning post, my way maker, and my company keeper. Holy God, I give you thanks because you know all about me and still love me without limits. Powerful God, out of my gratitude for how you have kept me, I give you thanks for _____ _____. Lord, your Word says, let the redeemed of the Lord say so. Thank you, God, that you not only redeemed my soul from an eternal hell *but my Great God you have redeemed me from __*

____ and I cannot thank you enough! And to the only true, Living God, with all I have and from the depths of my belly, I say thank you. Father, your Word says taste and see that the Lord is good. Holy One, I can bear witness because I have tasted and have seen that you are indeed good, and I offer thanksgiving to your name. In Jesus' name.

RUN with this today:

I am the *one* who turns back and says Thank you!

BONUS DEVOTIONAL
IT IS A CHOICE

I chose to be whole. Intentionality requires focus and a willingness to move toward a goal.

- Refuse to live broken in your heart!
- Refuse to live bitter in your soul!
- Refuse to go through life bruised and unhealed from your past!

When I chose to work through the hurts, pain, and mess I allowed myself to be a part of, the only way I came out was by being intentional. I had to decide I wanted a better life. I did not want to keep making the same bad decisions. I had to intentionally decide to pray and ask God to give me a brighter dream for my life. I am sharing the eight steps I used and still use in living my life intentionally.

Step 1: Make the choice. Choose what you are being intentional about. Make sure you are set on what you are choosing. Become attentive and immersed in the selection you have just made.

Step 2: Set measurable goals. Measurable goals include dates, times, and people that hold you accountable. Have a clear structure for reaching the goals.

Step 3: Become deliberate in reaching these goals.

Step 4: Read, pray, and seek help (pastors or mental health therapists) in reaching your goals of living whole.

Step 5: Develop checkpoints to ensure you stay the course as you work toward wholeness. Every month, review your goals, thoughts, words, and behaviors. Ensure everything is still aligning with your goal.

Step 6: Be kind to yourself. Examples: praying, massages, walks, meditating, or napping fifteen minutes daily as a quick reset.

Step 7: Write positive affirmations about being intentional. Set reminders on your phone that will send you a text message with positive affirmations for you to speak. Make yourself sticky notes with positive affirmations and place them in your car or in your home bathroom.

> *Examples of positive affirmations: I can do it; I am favored; Everything I touch is blessed; I am better than this; I am whole; I deserve more out of life; I am enough; or I am healthy in every area of my life.*

Step 8: Practice gratitude towards God and yourself. Tell the heavenly Father, thank you! Tell yourself thank you! Acknowledge your efforts, even if you have to start repeatedly.

My journey taught me that living a life of wholeness is not a one-and-done but a daily walk. But you are well able to overcome "it" (and whatever it is) and take possession!

Refuse to live broken in your heart! **Refuse** to live bitter in your soul! **Refuse** to go through life bruised and unhealed from your past!

Live blessed.

AFTERTHOUGHT

A couple of years ago, I asked my niece had her mom or dad told her when they would be leaving for a trip to Disney World. She told me, "I do not know, I just know dad said we would go before school opens in August. So, when my mom tells me to get my suitcase, I will know then Aunt Leatta!"

She had so much trust in her dad's words that she didn't even trouble herself with constant asking. She just trusted his words!

Listen, I know it's hard sometimes, but you must decide, even in those moments, to *judge God faithful who promised* (Heb. 11:11) like Sarah in the bible. You must know that He loves you. Understand God values His word and loves you too much. He cannot lie! Trust He is perfecting everything that concerns you!

Many hugs,

www.ingramcontent.com/pod-product-compliance
Lightning Source LLC
Chambersburg PA
CBHW070111080526
44586CB00013B/1262